DCJefferson
My wandering mind

Cover Design:
Publisher:
ISBN:
Printed in (Insert Country here)

First printing, 2020

Acknowledgment

The following pages you're about to experience is my first
endeavor into being an author. My Wandering Mind is
neither here nor there, but rather a realm in between my
mind, for I only know my mind and thoughts. I hope these
very personal thoughts may bring some peace of mind.

Dedication

This book is dedicated to my one and only soulmate
Caroline.

As I sit here and ponder the state of the world today, I feel empty. The emptiness of the feeling of a dream gone unfulfilled.

As I age and begin to realize my own mortality. It takes me into a deep, dark place of despair! A place where I don't want to be, yet I find myself constantly in that realm; the realm of uncertainty about life and death.

I often lose myself in a world of denial. Denial of what life has to offer, as life is for the living.

In a larger sense I'm not even remotely aware of who I am. I live in a world of total confusion and regret. I feel that this world as I know it is simply a moment in time that continues to run until there is no more.

In that time of being, that time of uncertainty, that time of doubt and self loathing, it is then that my wandering mind flourishes. I feel that no matter what I decide to change, that change may be predetermined no matter how I may try: my destiny is predestined.

I, me and myself do not always correlate on the same plane of thought.

My mind now finds itself thinking about what it would be like not to think. To not remember or carry the so-called memories within your soul or souls.

Soul or souls for me varies from day to day and is often unpredictable to a degree that causes me to look at me and say, why? Why do I think, why do I feel? What do I feel as if my mind spirals out of control to an abyss of meaningless thoughts, thoughts that I can never really understand or be able to convey in a manner for another to understand!

Understand? Understand what? He'll understand me. I'm that entity who refuses to accept the mental state of my own mind. My own self, the self that is me or is it? I dive deeply and completely to the mental images that scrolls and plays over and over in my mind in such a way that I don't know me.

Who am I? I am who? I am who, I am? Really, am I?

I, me and my is not able to fully conceive or accept what's here for me in this instance of being. A being of not reality at all but rather a reality built on what I feel this world should be.

This world? Should be my world, with my basic concept of reality being that I am what all should and eventually shall be! I have that mindfulness to take my sense of being to a level unknown to me. I am the me that lurks within the dark shadows of my mind, the shadows of disappointment and doubt. My shadow that's shrouded in my self being and loathing.

The turmoil and strife that evolves takes my mind to that space of not knowing. In that space I find me where I'm most unlikely to be within the thoughts and emotions of not knowing.

Not knowing what? Not knowing anything!

I sit here without the peace of mind that my mind so abundantly craves. In as much as I attempt to relate to the world and to life, I find myself constantly in doubt about what's really real. Am I real? How real am I? Do I simply exist within my own mind or is there a being that co-exists as me?

Thoughts? Why do I think thoughts if thoughts are but a figment of my own being? I, me and my still fails to come to a thorough understanding of what's me. I thrive to seek the true meaning of the world and my actual recommended or predestined part of it. It still being in an unknown state of mind, where I can evolve into it.

Mindlessness euphoric feelings of what I could be if I was me and my, and the provocation of thoughts that attempt to decipher what I want to be!

My mind suddenly phases into an abyss of unthinkable and unimaginable delusions. Delusions that I find both baffling but yet desirable, the desire that I hunger to be able to slide into another mental existence within my current being.

A being that's neither here nor there! A being that's able to morph into a place and space that's more adaptable to my inner feelings. Those feelings of me, my and I. I, me and my rebuke the awesomeness of the thoughts.

Why think? My mind is but a thought!

I'm now trying to make a correlation between my mind and myself. The darkening of my thoughts are only preceded by my deep desire to understand life. Life is what life is, but exactly what is life?

Think and think and think. I'm thinking yet there's no way to be sufficiently understood by me, my and I. At any rate, the delusion of happiness and success in this so-called life is vague at best.

I think, I think and I still can't ease my mind to sublimely find peace. A place that is as illusive as time.

Time? Time I may not have, for I can't seem to come to grips with the reality I find myelf in, a reality I fictionalize in my mind as not being real. Not being real what it seems to be.

To be or not to be is not an option within my deep, dark mind which searches for understanding of life for the living!

In my mind there is no place for patience. Patience in mind is patience in soul. My soul, my mind contains no patience. Life and death provides no patience.

I foresee within the depth of my soul, no need for patience. I, me and my want what I want as I want. The theoretical display of my memories as it relates to my being is surpassed by my desire to exist in mind, body and soul. What mind, what body, what soul? The reality of my mind do not have a desire or need for mind, body or soul. Yet in a larger sense and within the depths of my soul, may lie the peace of mind I seek with the patience I desire.

Within my heart, more so than in my mind, I seek patience. Patience that in all practicality does not exist within my soul. Patience is not patience!

Dark subtle thoughts invade my mind like a rabid dog, out of control yet into the now, the now of not knowing that hunger and thirst for understanding of where we are relative to the world in which we exist.

My world, my mind, my concepts, my delusions is but a figment of something deeper in my soul. My soul, as I contemplate the realness or rather the deceit, I find deep within the depth of my thinking. To think sometimes is to allow myself to escape into the dysfunctional and inept desire to hope.

I, me and my can't relate to the concept of hope. But picture as I may the illusiveness of hope that correlates within the legions of memories of my so-called life. For memories are but a collectiveness of my interactions and illusion of life!

In an attempt to superimpose life's thoughts of being in a realm that may not exist for me, I may not be evolving into a mental concept that me, my and I may not really exist. No, I'm not being gullible enough to accept some things in life on life turns.

What is life turns? Hell, what if life supposed to be for me? Interesting how I can be in a completely different mindset as I drift into the eerie world of dream world.

Am I dreaming?

My mind is in a constant turmoil, deciphering what's real and tangible for me. I perceive reality as reality plays out in my mind. I'm in control or am I?

The mind is a mythical subliminal world that not tangible for a delusional mind.

Am I being delusional?

What now? I'm struggling to get a thorough conception and not a deviation of where my mind tends to stray, to stray into a seemingless desire for more understanding of the unknown functioning of my mind without a memory.

For a memory only exists within my mind, therefore, I'm not sure if the reality this appears to be for a mind that's starved for more of me.

I slip most times into the dream world of the reality of what I think is life: what I think is life. That life for me, may not be. The delusional part of my mind says I'm the realness you seek. But am I thinking or dreaming?

Only my mind knows for sure!

My mind lives in a constant and unaware state of being, a being that leads me to think about the unthinkable existing of matter and space. That matter and space contains my most inner thoughts and most undesirable fears.

Fears of not understanding me, my and I as my mind palpitates into an even deeper concept of non-reality, it refuses to accept or be willing to endure that deep, dark existence where I live in my mind!

A life I find intriguing and still misleading. A misleading of possible trauma implemented and transplanted deep into my conscious and unconscious by a mind that's fragile at best.

Fragile? Yes fragile but not yet broken am I. Mind over memories? Is that even possible for me?

I remain constant and unware inside of my illusion of living this life as one of the living!

So now I find myself in the throes of yet another unknown foe that lives within my mind. Or is it within my memories?

Those memories have the ability to intrude and add conflicted understanding of what I may or may not be thinking. It may serve me, my and I best that the elusive and unknown foe be eradicated by depressing memories while they cling to the bonds of my mind.

If there is another attack on my saneness by that which lies within the columns of memories, it will only confirm and rectify the unknown of self. That self is suspended between the here and now, today and yesterday!

Yet I seek tomorrow.

Tomorrow is the illusiveness of the mind that never is able to quite manifest itself in me, my and I. Is it even possible to corral a possible unit of time, as that time constantly rolls and flows into another dimension?I feel an emptiness as my mind struggles with the acceptance of it as that may be.

Me, my and I don't tolerate the conflict of the mind and memory by simply rejecting both. Rejecting yet not bending to either or neither!

Mind, memory and self is but an opportunity to utilize that which is unknown as a strategy to being of this instance. This instance of time will never coherently be able to ever occur again as I may know it, however, within my mind it may manifest itself into a being that me, my and I may not be oblivious to.

At any rate, I find myself lost and all alone in my own self being that apparently can't distingue the mind as opposed to the memories. My mind tells me to think of memories that's currently consuming my thoughts as an obstacle without obstacles, for I am now allowing my memories to manifest into a more mental place within me.

A place as frightful to me, my and I, as being unable to reconcile the tangible realness in my world from fictitious rhetoric, I shall forever be of the mindset that above all, that may seem to possess my soul, I am still me and my!

The reality I seek attempts to manifest itself into a deep darkened space and place, where the only issue is reality itself. I still allow my inner most self to plunge deeper and deeper into some realm of realization that's not really real. Not real because I choose to let me and my to become as one but not together.

No togetherness to cloud my mind and my judgment to exist without me to truly recognize the hypothesis of my ways!

Yes I do and don't understand or choose not to understand the actuality of myself as I constantly search for my being. That being I still struggle to comprehend, a being that may transpose itself into a new dimension within my mental existence.

If I can't comprehend the reality of it all, then my mind will be in a constant state of purgatory. Being in a space and time that may only exist in my mind I try to make a vail attempt to understand this life, to understand this world and to understand me, my and I.

As more often than not, my memories of life have gone by and counteracts my inward emotional toll to perceive me and life. Life and me may entwine, but it is in an optional dimension that I can't control.

It is a wanting within my mind to co-exist with my life and my memories to the point that it may take me to a deeper illusion of myself. That illusion of me may manifest itself deeper into my mind and explore the memories of my life.

Whirlwinds of memories twirl within my being, taking me to a time and space I crave to somehow recreate as if I could turn back time. Time that has gone by in that instance super imposes itself into a memory.

It is a memory that I may be forced to alter in a way to suit my desire for the understanding of life on so-called life terms. Be that as it may, I, me and my will forever be linked into the haze of memories of days gone by, days that had no definitive rationale for invading my thoughts.

I think the thought of the memory of the thought as though that thought will expand my thoughts.

I think...

Well, my mind as usual has begun the endless journey to find meaning within a source of no means. I attempt to disguise the true memory in an attempt to fortify my inner being of self. That self still can't exemplify the existence of the memories that tend to lurk so deep and darkly within my soul.

My soul is tied to the memories of mind and being in such a complex entwinement that it leaves me confused but yet able to comprehend that which I seek and that which eludes me, is now a peace of mind, as well as the peace to understand my life and the memories that correlate to each other.

I'm not even sure if what I attempt to rationalize as a memory is really life. Life is a word that I envision living but how do I live within myself?

Now the emotional side of me, my and I is attempting to reconcile the thought of the memories and the memories of the thoughts of a life that is seeming unfilled with the conjuring of a space where I find myself running from myself. Or running somewhere that may or may not exist in the realm of my mind's deepest thoughts of rationale.

As sure as day follows the night my mind still struggles in between to factor if I want the darkness or the light. In as much as I can conceive the images of thoughts and memories gone by, I still have an issue with my mind being able to recollect that instance. It is an instance I will never experience again, even if my mind told me to understand the objective of me, my and I.

To recall the memories of the life that's gone by me, it may take more of an effort than I could possibly filter within the depths of my mind.

It is a mind that's so overly abundant with doubt and disbelief in the memories that tend to creep ever so slowly into my being. That of a being to have no desire or rather no reason to desire to recall the memories of life's roads.

Roads that went somewhere but yet in another sense, those roads led to nowhere that I can recall within the memories or the thoughts of my being. That being of me, my and I.

Am I really alive for life or is life alive for me?

For the most part of my mental capacity to indulge my memories of life, or my life of memories, is pale in comparison to what I somehow can't quite comprehend or conjure a mental representation of the memories of the life I choose to not conquer.

For if I was able to really conquer that vision of my memories of my, me and I as it's relative to the here and now of life, I would then be unable to grasp the reality of it all.

It is the reality of the visions as they're somehow transplanted within the memories of a life suspended, a life suspended in the disbelief of this memory of life or thoughts that entwine as one combustible unknown entity.

This is an entity that still eludes me. It eludes my and most definitely eludes the I that may not really exist.

In an effort to find some solitude within myself, my mind, more often than not, finds an optional sense of being. Those options, though deep in meaning, brings no meaning to myself as I still attempt to unravel the meaning of the life of my memory.

It is a life that manifests itself into a true memory or rather just a fleeing thought. My thoughts still haunt me as if the memory of the thoughts was somehow superimposed in my conscious being.

That is within the degree of consciousness between the time and space of the memory and the thought. I wholeheartedly embrace that realm of the unknown in an attempt to find some sanctuary for my mind to be at rest.

That is the most needed escape which allows me to hide in plain sight of myself and I.

And so I contemplate what the memories of the thoughts of the memory are, that I may be thinking into existence, even though the memory does not really exist. Now my most deepest and darkest thoughts sprout up as to tell me that I'm still not able to bring to reality the inner me that I choose not to exhibit to me.

My is still seeking me and I is a figment of my imagination or is it really? Think the thoughts or live the memories? I can't quite come to terms with either since the thoughts or the memories both tend to still elude my understanding of myself. Myself is not the self that I think or the me my soul seeks!

Let the me, my and I exist as separate entities or let them merge into confusion.

I'm beginning to wander into another world that my thoughts interjected within my mind. My mind is attempting to reconcile with the unknown world or the unknown thought by which it was manifested. However, within my mind I find an evolving force that makes me hunger for more understanding of my thoughts and my memories as one.

One, not in each other but one in equal but separate portions, is in my imagination. That imagination somehow finds a crevice to ease itself into my self consciousness even when I attempt to reject that entity from my vessel.

The vessel of myself being that I must, at all costs, attempt to preserve and yet reserve the thoughts of the memories as well as the memories of the thoughts.

At this time I find myself lost and locked into my inner feelings of thoughts about the memories I choose not to remember for fear of a reckoning within my soul. My soul is impulsive as free flowing thoughts, flowing deep and yet deeper into nothing.

Nothing because I'm still living in a hope for a new way to understand me, my and I. I could say that me don't know my. Yet, I can't understand the rationale that's necessary to distinguish the memory from the thought. My memory makes me choose to not remember the thought as the thought does not exist without the said memory.

My innermost desire to understand the unknown median we call thoughts implodes into memories. Are those memories for me, my or I?

As me, my and I do not co-exist in an effort to reduce my thoughts into subliminal memories, I allow myself to gingerly inhabit the depths of my soul yet again. My soul is not to be even remotely associated with my mind and memories.

My soul is a time and place that exists only when there is an issue that necessitates its presence.

In its presence I'm there yet I'm not, really. I visualize the struggle between memories and thoughts as one makes a feeble attempt to influence the other. Now in my mind I allow no dominance of mind or memory.

I often allow my mind to drift into a place and time that I don't recognize by choice or is it me, my and I refusing to conjure up the existence of the memories as I thoughtfully attempt to understand me.

The me that can so easily be lost in the valleys of my mind as if to emulate a memory of a thought of the memory is really not there. As far as living the life that produces for an unsteady way while constantly streaming said memories of moments in time has gone awry.

Today my mind is no mind that I know. I lost myself monetarily and slipped back into yesterday's illusions of grandeur. It serves me, my and I no good to offer a frail attempt of fantasizing thoughts of the memories.

The memories that inhibit my very soul believe that the thoughts of the memories are real. Real they may be in the thoughts of that memory, but not within the depths of my being.

My mind...

Thinking about the thoughts only causes me to think about the memories I choose not to remember. My choice for me and I is to fabricate partial memories of the thoughts that I think when I think of the thoughts I choose to think. Still, I find myself lost to even conjure up a memory of a thought that I aim to think about.

My thoughts, as mindful as they may be, can't quite convince me of the reality of my memories. Memories of the thoughts in mind lead way to an underlying issue, with being able to think up said memories and then transform that memory into a thought.

It is a thought filled with all of the mystery of the unknown sector of memories within my mind that I think up.

To be me, my and I takes more of being out of mind more so than embracing the memories here within. For within the deepness of my unconsciousness, I repel away all memories of the thoughts and all thoughts of the memories.

I'm now within a new existence of memories of the mind, as I make a useless attempt to savage a thought. A thought when my desire is not to think? What thinking of such thoughts of the memories that is that I don't want to think about?

My mind is lost deeply into a sequence of thoughts of memories or is it memories of thoughts?

My mind...

Within my being of my memories of my mind, I can't really distinguish me, my and I at times. Those are the times when my mind, more often than not, chooses not to remember the memories of the thoughts.

They are thoughts of the memories that haunt me like a bad dream. A dream of a world with no thoughts or memories. My mind is struggling to not remember or not think about the memories of the thoughts. Yet my mind, at times, tends to drift back into a world of memories when I only desire thoughts.

Thoughts of me, my and I.

I try to engage with me and my in a way that do not require memories or thoughts as I choose not to. With that choice my mind is in a steady disarray as to how to exist.

Mindful with thought or mindful with memories? The answer to that question still, and probably will, always elude me. My mind operates as if I'm not in control of my thoughts or of my memories.

Alas, my mind is not mindful of the illusion and grandeur of being able to not memorize thoughts of the memories. Thoughts that causes me, my and I to think in an unknown spectrum of memories that I choose not to remember.

As my life entwines within my soul, my mind can't discern the memories of the thoughts that still fail to manifest itself within me, my and I. Why is my mind the way it is or the way it is, is in my mind?

Withstanding the illusions of yesterday, today and tomorrow, my mind is struggling to decipher where I want to be at this time. Today is full of memories of yesterday which is more memories of thoughts. Tomorrow may not truly exist as that span of time evolves into memory thoughts for today.

Yesterday? It never existed in my, me and I's mind as I look for tomorrow in today!

In solitude I engage in a mental desire to understand me, my and I co-existing as one, not three. I still let the internal struggle of memories versus thoughts consume my mindful or mindless desire to find peace.

That peace of mind would allow me to not only recognize me, my and I, but to also ease my true realization of each. I often allow myself to be misunderstood in the realm of the memories.

The thoughts? Well, at this level of existence, the thoughts may be the memories.

Or it may be not!

Here I go again. Finding myself lost yet again in the same struggle. Memories versus thoughts. I just can't quite comprehend or even recommend to me, myself or I, for I am in a space and place right now that befuddles me to say the very least.

I am who I am or am I me?

The me that still wants to exist and not in either realm of yesterday, tomorrow or even today! Today is the one constant that I do have, however, it's not the consistency I'm seeking, but rather the peace of mind.

Where does that peace lie? I want and will always reject the thoughts of the memories. The memories of the thoughts I reject.

I think that I think to much about thinking about why I think. Yet the memories ease into said thoughts that I'm not truly thinking about. I ask myself if what I'm thinking is a memory or a thought? I don't think I know. If I did know, then the memory of me thinking will not let a thought manifest itself in my mind.

My mind appears as dark as the night or as brilliant as the early morning sunrise. That sunrise will surely be followed by a sunset, but will I be thinking about it or having a memory of it?

As that internal debate looms in my soul, I really don't think I need to remember.

My soul is as mindful as my thoughts of memories. I cling to the hope that I will become more aware of my mind as it sways like a tree in the wind, bending but not breaking. I still suffer the same insecurities of my memories that are relative to my thoughts.

Will I ever be able to really define and refine my memory of the thoughts of me, my and I? I can't even begin to decipher all of the feelings that's implanted deep within the memory of my thoughts.

For most times, I don't even think of the thought of the memory as I make a frail attempt to reconcile the three entities that is me, my and I.

Mind, memories and thoughts. My mind is thinking of the thoughts that I'm not ready to remember in as much as I don't want to forget as well. The turmoil inside my head is constantly adding more insight into me, my and I.

I really feel like the deepest, the most humble of emotions can still cause me to regret. Regret the lost or purged memories of the thoughts I choose not to want to remember.

As I exercise my mental capacity to accept and devise a more understandable reason for the desire to forget the thought of the memories I start to devise a more inner me.

I often sit and contemplate how I could better understand me and my memories of the thoughts of the thoughts. I think in an effort to control the influx of memories of the thoughts that I can't convince myself to be real needs to be addressed.

Real to me takes on a totally different meaning inside my head. I'm trying to explore the very depths of my thoughts and why do I think of them. Should I still elect to let the memories overthrow the thoughts? Am I able to proactively assume that the thoughts and the memories is possible and one in the same?

I, me and my don't think so. I'm thinking about it.

My mind has now taken my thoughts of my memories to a totally bizarre space deep within a world of confusion. That confusion makes me cling more to denial of the being of me, my and I to be relative to the memories of my thoughts.

I most definitely feel a need to dig deeper within my cortex to examine the memories and thoughts. I can't seem to be able to relate to the unknown vision of self.

It is those auras of visionless memories that I so desperate shy away into from another perception of me, my and I.

My mind is foggy with thoughts that I didn't think of and memories of instances I didn't experience. I'm lost and fighting within myself to somehow understand and wade through all of the turmoil my mind sends my way.

As I think the thoughts, I'm feeling flabbergasted for I can't explain what I'm thinking. Thinking of the memories that I don't remember only serves to further exploit my thoughts about said memories.

In a sense, me, my and I is but an illusion that I chose to render into my current self. I have no way to really express the internal battle between me, my and I.

How do I reconcile my thoughts of the vision of the memories as it relates to my desire to dive yet deeper into the ball of confusion? I yield to the confusion as I feel helpless to control my thoughts.

In another wasted effort, I attempt yet again to try and understand me, my and I. The realization of it all comes down to control my mind, as my mind centers around me.

I'm entirely consumed with the realization of the mental life that dwells within the thoughts of those memories. With very little recollection of my thoughts as they are relative to my being as a vapor.

Yes, a vapor of hope that dissolves ever so quickly away. Far away is me, my and I most times. I don't feel like muddling up those memories or thoughts as they too evaporate into nothing.

I indeed fail in my most futile attempt to regain some level of understanding that in me, my and I, may appear to be three entities but in reality, we're all one.

One in a multitude of misconceptions about each other. Those misconceptions tend to move me deeper into a realm of disbelief in myself.

In that, what's constant within the depths of my complicated existence in mind, I can't find me or my mind!

Life is but a moment in time, but a time, and space that really exists only if I can recall the memories. For without the memories of the thoughts, did the event actually happen for me?

Me, my and I still can't absorb the deep dark place where my mind normally inhabits with a lot of confusion.

Now more so than ever, my mind is drifting yet again into a realm of solitude that causes me to be rendered thoughtless. Being thoughtless will afford me to mentally reject the memories by not thinking. Not thinking requires a degree of self discipline that causes me yet more confusion of self.

Me, my and I transform into a vessel of discontent mixed with self idealization of my memory of the thoughts. I become more adapt to wading through the memories in yet another futile effort to self explore. Explore that internal or eternal being of self.

As I still dig deeper into that part of my memories, perhaps I can manifest it into my thoughts. Why think? Do I think?

Me, my and I repels thinking.

Lately I find my mind whispering itself into a dimension of a place I know not. Or do I?

The places and spaces I've been still haunt me like a rabid dog. I find myself attempting yet again to justify the thoughts that I think, and thinking about why I'm thinking about what I'm thinking about?

I'm lost in a mental state of semi disbelief that life for me, my and I, exists. Or does that life really exist or am I living within my conceptual being within my mind?

Within a mind rich in imagination of real things that are not real.

I sometimes allow my mind to gently weep with the thought of memories that I thought about yesterday but yet to recall them today! Why is there no recall for me?

I and my refuses to let me enjoy the thought of the memories as I attempt to suppress even more of the memories and thoughts that I just don't want! I just don't want thoughts or memories of yesterday, today or even tomorrow.

My mind is just as elusive as a thief in the night. I can not and will not allow my mental capacity to consume me, my and I.

My mind, my thoughts and my memories are but segments of time that have come and gone, only to return to my being as if it never left my soul. I can't keep running rapidly from that soul which is within the depths of my heart since it relates to allowing myself the opportunity to try to understand me, my and I.

I desire to engage my thoughts into a new realm of being that allows for me to distinguish the thought from the memory. I still think deeply about how I struggle, yet even more so to deal with the reality of being and the reality of acceptance of oneself and one's memories and thoughts.

Again, I shall not embrace either mindfully.

Why do I think about things that I can't come to terms with as I'm not even sure of my being? I and me still feels suspended in a world of mystical being.

Memories and thoughts. Thoughts and memories. I consider it one in the same some of the times.

For my mind is never content with the pattern of thinking about past memories, I want to suppress and not think of it.

In as much as I try to compel myself to think only about nothing and nothing about thinking, I'm thinking of the memories within the memory of the thoughts that I was thinking.

Now I'm thinking thoughts about thinking about thoughts. I'm not able to capture the me, my and I within a realization that all of them do exist within my mind.

it is my mind that struggles with the reality of life and the reality of myself. In my mind the realness is diluted by memories of thoughts of times when I couldn't really think.

Who am I?

Rarely, with most moments, I don't know who I am or what my purpose of being here is as I tend to live within my mind in my own conjured up mystical world. I just pretend that I exist for the realm I'm in which may not be as real as I think or thought!

I need to stop thinking thoughts for mentally my thoughts are memories of things I was thinking of in the middle of a thought.

My mind, my thoughts and my memories is a cluster of self doubt and loathing. As I think about me and my, I'm still not certain which is which.

Am I me or am I my?

My mind is so elevated into the misery of the unknown that I can't even control my mind as it wonders off into oblivion. I still look at me and my in a fruitless attempt to seek to ease the pain of the thoughts of the memories that I don't want to think.

Thinking hinders my consciousness to the point that the mere task of thinking up a thought causes me to lose control of my mind and allow it to simply exist.

I'm about to exit reality and live within my mind, a mind where I don't know me. I don't know my soul reason for living in thoughts of memories that I still do not embrace or even want to remember.

Deep down inside me, my and I will never co-exist, for within my mind is no mind or memories at all.

As I come to the realm of attempting to understand, yet still understand the why about the memories of the thoughts, I find myself as a wandering mind!

About the Author

With a Bachelor of Arts in Radio and Television Production, including a Minor in Photo-Journalism, DC Jefferson has been an on air-announcer for several years on several radio stations before settling into corporate America.

DC Jefferson sought out to pursue new creative interests, which lead him to discover the beauty of the written word. Now armed with a passion for this new endeavor, DC Jefferson has found inspiration within himself and others.

For more information about DC Jefferson, you can find him on (https://www.facebook.com/ Dennis Jefferson.

Made in the USA
Middletown, DE
06 November 2020